Y0-ELU-159

BEAR THE PALL

Stories & Poems about the Loss of a Parent

> **Pall**
> *noun*
> 1. a cloth, often of velvet, for spreading over a coffin, bier, or tomb.
> 2. a coffin.
> 3. anything that covers, shrouds, or overspreads, especially with darkness or gloom.

*T K M*co
The Kelly Mercantile Company

Bear the Pall
Published in 2015 by The Kelly Mercantile Company
Edited by Sally K Lehman

Copyrights (c) The Authors
ISBN:9781508547075

"Our Hell" by Sally K Lehman was previously published
in Perceptions: A Magazine of the Arts, 2014

Bear the Pall

Introduction
by Sally K Lehman

My Mom died. It's a simple sentence – noun, past tense verb, possessive form of the word I. The mother belonging to me has ceased to live. Seems easy enough. Parents are supposed to die before their children, it's that whole circle of life thing, but it's not until you can say that simple three word sentence that you really understand what it means.

When your mother or father dies, you can't ask them any more questions, you can never again hear the stories you grew up with, Mother's Day and Father's Day have a new pause to them. You can't stand up to them and ask why they did the things that you knew, even as a child, were wrong. And the impact of losing your parent brings up the complete range of emotions – sorrow, yes, but also guilt, relief, and even anger.

We have so many ways to say that someone we love died. Angels carried him away, she bit the big one, breathed her last, crossed over, departed, gave up the ghost, kicked the bucket, lost his life, passed away, is resting in peace. All of these reference loss and peace for the person who is gone. What they do not take into consideration are the people left here, taking care of the little details of disassembling another person's life, then learning to go on without that person. And if that person is someone you have known literally for your forever, one of the people who made you and raised you and explained things *like* death to you?

No one tells us how to keep breathing after our parent is gone.

The writers who have shared their stories and poetry here are amazingly honest about their experiences. Reading their words helped me in my own understanding of my emotional reactions to the death of my mother. And, yes, even through the anger.

So, I thank these writers and poets for their willingness to share one of the most difficult things in life. I encourage you to read all of their words and wisdom, if not for today than for one day when you will face what we have faced.

Hate

by Rene Mullen

I hate having to say good-bye,
I hate having never said good-bye.
That my head knows but my heart
doesn't seem to care.
That my heart cares but my head
remembers.
That I couldn't see past your illness,
your beatings,
your apathy,
your internal struggles,
or your lack of care for mine.
I hate that people hated you
before you were laid down to rest.
I hate that they tell me to love you
for who you weren't,
for who my heart still wishes you were.
I hate you for leaving,
every time you left.
I hate me for letting you come back.
I hate you for putting me in this position.
I hate me for making you put me in this position.
I hate that some day I'll end
up in the same bed you did, dying
of broken innards and a bleeding heart.
I hate that I couldn't get past the things
you did to me.
I hate that you're my father.
I hate that I'm a terrible son.

Assurance
by Miriam Pederson

It wasn't until after Mom died
that he had real things to say to me—
only daughter, perhaps his final confessor.
I think I listened like Mother—
half distracted, thinking about the disorder
of his book case, or what to make for dinner
while he quoted scripture
or tried to clear his throat.
Yet, his once competent hands
took me to a place so deep
that nothing can describe its hold on me:
the way he opened a bible, held an infant in baptism,
measured wood before he cut,
a steady certainty, as in a hymn,
its chords and promises
of blessed assurance.

When infirmities of his body
admitted questions and fears
into the rooms of his heart,
I could feel the shaking,
the clumsy efforts to hold on.
It was then I know I loved him best,
in the pale imprecise light of his final faith.

Memorial Day : Oregon 2002
by Miriam Pederson

What to remember on this day
unsoiled so far by the past?
Here we are, perched on a mountain,
a bullfrog's low strum from the millpond,
my most tender brother
making our coffee, humming.
Late morning we hike the Lumberman's Road
with our father whose walking stick
sets our gravelly pace.
We remark in our city voices on the view,
the sky soon frowning
a thunderbolt upon the family group.

A sliver so thin, it enters unfelt
and then the twinge, the shudder—
our mother gone,
her voice not even an echo.
Keeping the rhythm,
our expert shoes are wearing thin,
my brother's handsome profile
against the darkening sky.
We are making our way to the spring
where water rises before us
in a gush like sorrow overflowing--
her face, her long arms around us,
herself now a mist in the distance,
ourselves beginning the return
back to our lives down the mountain
back to the place before this day began.

Drawing Down
   by Kate Redmond

The first time Mom told me she had some kind of serious health issue and was handling it through Christian Science, she conveyed it with such calm and peace I did not process the message at all. She wouldn't have wanted to offer physical details, and I knew not to ask. Really, all I heard was that I wasn't to worry, she was working with her practitioner, love, calm, peace, joy, no worry.

When my sister called me six months later at Christmas to demand why I'd kept Mom's cancer from her for so long, I was truly flummoxed. I'd had no idea I was keeping a secret.

"But, she said she told you last summer!"

"What? No! That she had cancer?! No! Wait…" I racked my brain. "She told me there was something that she was handling but that I wasn't to worry! I mean, the way she talked about it – she was so calm and I didn't … I just didn't get it. I didn't even think anything of it!"

"Well, she has cancer."

~~~

If I'd known what melanoma looked like I'd have seen it when she visited us in Jakarta the last time – even then she wasn't keen to walk barefoot on the sand, and she wore socks with her Birkenstocks in the equatorial heat. I guess I do remember a weird brown splotch on her foot.

Mom's physical symptoms were not the point. They're never the point with Christian Scientists. And the physical aspects of Mom's well-being never worried me much.

I worried that she was a narcissist.

I worried that she was alone.

I worried that she took herself too seriously, because she was a narcissist and alone.

I worried she felt closer to her pets than me and my children and I worried that she felt fine about that.

I worried that I wasn't a good daughter; I worried about the things I knew about her that I wish I never knew; and I worried that what she knew about me prevented her from seeing me at my full measure. I worried she held on to her image of me at my worst self just as, in my worst moments, I could not stop seeing her at her most flawed. And I was furious that my mother should hold me to any version of myself at all – mothers are meant to see the best in their children, to adore them and to help them see the best in themselves.

When I lived nearby, I worried over holidays, almost unable to ask if she had somewhere to be on Christmas, on Thanksgiving, Easter. We made efforts to be together, though these were always small gatherings limited to just us and they felt paltry. None of us had any money and Mom tried not to seem put-upon to provide the meals.

During my mother's illness, I lived overseas with my husband Craig and our boys, so then it was down to my sister and to Mom's friends to see that she was covered over the holidays. I say that as if Mom had no say in the matter and, of course, she did; she was an adult in charge of her own life. But she was alone.

We never talked about the worst of all the holidays. My little brother, Sprig, died on Mother's Day when he was two years old. We could not make Mother's Day okay.

Dad left eight years after Sprig died. My sister and I were wrecked by the tragedy of Mom's life. We tried to make our love be enough, but we were never enough to stop her from wailing in her room, vomiting after meals, sighing at the breakfast table. We weren't enough to make her better, and we weren't enough to merit her making herself better so that she could take care of us.

So we grew up taking care of her or raging against having to take care of her. We tried to be easy. We told her all the time how pretty she was and that we loved her. For years she relied on our kindness and support, and when we couldn't manage it, she withdrew into sobbing or grim disappointment.

It was impossible to make right all the injustices in our mother's life, and to be attentive and kind constantly.

~~~

For most of my adult life, I waxed solicitous and waned dismissive. I felt terrible for her and then angry at having to worry about her. I worried about her, about her well being, her loneliness, her past sorrows and whether her current strengths were enough to bring her comfort. I worried that she was alone all the time, that she would always be alone without the comfort of being known and cherished.

The extent to which I did not do enough for her staggers me.

~~~

When she was dying I held my mother in bed, spooned against her back, and I felt her sigh into my embrace. And then she murmured, "Thank God for Craig."

I wondered if she meant thank God I had married someone so good, who loved me. And then I thought no, she means thank God for Craig who sees her without my filter of pity, guilt, judgment and remorse. Craig thought she was wonderful, hilarious, admirable. He delighted in her.

Mom radiated life. She skied fast and beautifully. She mountain biked at top speeds over steep terrain. She snowboarded. She windsurfed. She was a climber – that's how she met our Dad. And after he left us, she took her two daughters and nieces on week-long backpacking trips. Not long after I started driving, we dropped her by herself at a trailhead in the Sawtooths and she emerged sixty miles and five days later. She rode her bike solo to San Diego from Boise. She was remarkable and we admired her and wished she had the capacity to mother us.

Mom was greatly loved in her community. She worked in a high profile position – she was known as the "face" of the ski area. She remembered names, asked about family, clasped shoulders, gave warm hugs, laughed and commiserated. She helped found the local animal shelter; she served on the Chamber of Commerce. She sang in a local choir and volunteered at the Special Olympics.

Mom loved her larger than life reputation. She loved being known and beloved in her community. And she had many very close and dear friends. It must have been burdensome to be loved through such cracked and clouded filters as those of her daughters.

As an adult I took her to task. I held Mom accountable for leaving us, for joking with friends at our expense, for neglecting my little sister, for taking glamorous jobs at the ski area that kept her away from home all the time instead of finding a way to work and still take care of us.

Mom took it.

She said, "I wish I could have it all to do again."

She said, "I took the typing test to become a temp or a secretary and I couldn't pass it! I didn't think I could do anything else."

She was sorry for our anger and hurt and she was brave about making us understand that she was not going to allow us to freeze her in time as that person. She took responsibility for having left us to ourselves, and she asked us to join her right now in the present moment. She was brave to take our anger. She was committed to growing and changing as a person. She was a little ahead of us in that. My sister and I couldn't ever wholly let go of our wrecked childhoods.

Still the three of us - me, Mom, and my sister - were always swinging the words "I love you" like grappling hooks, hoping to catch hold.

~~~

I was relieved when Mom made it clear she was handling her situation through Christian Science. I knew that would be a comfort to her. If she were to be healed, then, what joy, what gratitude. That would be a terrific celebration. And if not, she'd go with integrity, in keeping with her beliefs. And anyway, she lived in the mountains. It was far too late for chemotherapy and the nearest hospital was two hours away. She couldn't have made the drive on her own.

Of course she'd have had dozens of volunteers, but that wasn't the real point. The point was that Mom wanted to have her life, her own life, not the misery, pain, sickness and dependence of chemo. For her, it was either rely on prayer and stay in her home living her life, expecting healing, or give up and subject herself to the misery and indignity of treatment.

I felt like a traitor for not also being a Christian Scientist, for leaving her to it. Over that year, all of us saw that Mom's prayerful work brought a tremendous peace to her. She was deeply connected to the divine. It would have been hard to credit, and also somehow not at all a surprise, if she had been healed.

When I flew back from Jakarta to see Mom just a month before she passed away, she shimmered around the edges, both lifting away and impatiently tethered to her earthly form. She was aware of the process, and seemed torn between desiring healing on this earthly plane and preparing herself to transcend it.

I don't know if death confers some sudden wisdom. I suppose it does. Just as giving birth cracks your heart open with love you never knew you were capable of feeling, the passage itself must open access to higher understanding. In that regard, to my mind Mom had her healing.

When we called her for comfort or support, Mom would say to us that we are all always enveloped in Love; we cannot be removed from ever-present divine Love. There is nowhere that Love isn't. Armed with this understanding, we do not dwell on what is missing; indeed, we look to what is: the abundance of Love that is our birthright. I wonder why I didn't imagine that she offered herself the same comfort with all the prayerful work that she did over the years.

~~~

"Oh honey," I can hear her breathe in her warm voice. "Honey, you only saw through your understanding. You had Craig," and here her voice softens.

"You had Craig and Craig's family and those two wonderful boys. But I wouldn't have wanted all those people around!"

She laughs, knowing it's as much an insult as an attempt to comfort.

"I loved getting up early and making coffee, reading the Lesson in bed. I loved walking with my dog Dali right out to the bird refuge, and coming home to my little house in this beautiful meadow. I loved seeing my friends when I wanted to see them, and being alone when I wanted to be alone!"

If she could today, she would take my hand.

~~~

When my sister and I imitate Mom now on the phone we use this same gentle, loving voice. We laugh and we both say that is so comforting to hear.

"Kate," Mom would say, "I'm good."

***Everything roars, and
everything falls silent.***
by Emily Shearer

It is not enough to bear the pall. Bearing the pall
is to resurfacing what glitter is to
a universe of stars.
To spit the earth, choke the throat
of fire, brave the pressing weight
of a guidance you can't follow,
and garner the raging hope of a million hungry orphans.

That's step one.

Thief, I Know Your Name
by Emily Shearer

Upon re-entering the country of my birth,
I found all the locks broken;
my entire homeland strip-mined
yet the criminal remained unsentenced and at large,
free to rampage, free to wrest children from their mothers' arms
and mothers from their grown daughters' breakfast nooks,
family outings, commemorations.

Though my gut aches to condemn,
occupation so fully realized cannot be confined
to one cell
Her ovaries, breast, brain,
my heart, my breath, my despair.
Predaceous stranger guilefully spares nothing,
and I, gangly ablated thing, cut off from placental oxygen
spare my faith in its marauding wake.

Thief, I know your name.

A Child's Hurt
  by Tina V. Cabrera

I am a child. It is May 1977. I am eight years old and Mama is
sitting on the couch next to Papa holding a letter in her hands,
leaning towards Papa like she is going to fall onto his shoulder.

Papa speaks for Mama. Papa says that Grandma has died. But
Mama is not crying. Just one sound comes from her mouth, just
one great big wail and her mouth is open. I think Mama is in pain,
but I don't see any tears.

When Mama comes back from burying Grandma in the Philippines
– my Grandma whom I never met – she brings back pictures. I see
the picture of Grandma in a black coffin, and her face is all
powdery with white powder on it. The coffin is big and Grandma
is big, wearing a black and white spotted fur coat. Mama says she
died of a heart attack, and that she ate and ate and ate herself to
death because she was sad that her husband died many years
ago. I turn away from the picture of Grandma in the coffin
because it frightens me. I do not feel any pain and I do not cry
over Grandma. Mama used to read letters from Grandma that
came from Manila, letters that said hello to us kids and that she
missed us. But I wonder how she can miss me when she never
met me and I wish I'd met Grandma and I wish I could cry for her.

Mama puts the pictures of Dead Grandma in the same photo
album of Young Grandma. She puts Dead Grandma in the back
and keeps Young Grandma in the front —so that when you turn
the pages of the photo album, you can see Grandma grow old. I
look at the pictures and I can't believe that Grandma in the black
coffin is the same Grandma in golden dresses with her face and
hair all dolled up. Real pretty, like Mama in her old pictures. And

real thin. But in the coffin she's real big and her face is swollen. At the same time that I want to look at the picture, I don't want to look at the picture. I'm afraid of the grey face behind the white powder and the large, very large body.

~~~

I am twenty-nine years old and I am still a child. Mama dies. I am in pain and I cry. At first, Papa and I refuse to look at Mama in the casket. We want to remember her the way she was. But then we do look in the casket, and she looks like she's only sleeping. They did a good job. Made her look real pretty with bright red lipstick painted on her lips, just how she likes it.

My sister Dyna asks if I want to see the pictures – the ones she took of Mama in the pink coffin. I say that's okay. I don't want to. Even though she looked pretty in the coffin when I saw her, I can't look at the pictures. It feels like when Papa and I first went home, after the funeral service; I was afraid to walk inside the house, without Mama there, and when I did step inside, the air felt stiff and cold.

To this day I haven't seen those pictures of Mama in the pink coffin. And I never will. I will never lay the picture of Grandma in her black coffin next to Mama in her pink one.

Ashes To Ashes
    by Debi Knight Kennedy

Mom and I looked nothing alike. She was tall to my short, thin to my thick, her skin fair and her eyes blue where mine are olive-toned and hazel. The very structure of our facial bones couldn't be more different. No one, ever, assumed we were related. Not even at family reunions. The big ones where nobody really knows who anybody else is, you all just look like you belong there; I am usually asked who I came with.

And yet, now that she is gone, something quite remarkable has been happening.

At first it scared me. I thought grief was causing me to imagine things. It wasn't so much the feeling of Mom's face inhabiting my own, that part was nice, like she was with me. It was the time I looked in the mirror and saw her looking back that I thought I might be going crazy.

Another time it happened at the Thai Cottage, where I was having lunch with my sister, over a steaming platter of crispy egg rolls with plum sauce. I had felt it coming on, the face thing, but was getting used to it by then so didn't think much of it. For my sister though, it was quite a shock. She stopped eating, an egg roll half way in and half way out of her mouth, to stare at me.

"What's the matter," I said.

"This is going to sound really weird," she said, "but you look like Mom right now."

"I know," I said. "I can feel her in my face. She does that sometimes. I think she's saying hello."

We never spoke of it again. At least now I knew that I wasn't crazy. Whatever was happening might be unexplainable but it was real.

Despite my mom's early conservatism, by the time she was in her seventies she was open to all kinds of wild ideas. We talked about most everything, from sex to drugs to the great beyond. How we might communicate from 'the other side' was one of our favorites, though she always made me promise that she was going to be the one doing the communicating with me. I was absolutely not allowed to die first. We talked about how we wanted to go, agreed that when our times came we would both like to be surrounded by women who would sing us out of this world and into the next. We spoke of cremation versus burial, church service versus celebration of life.

Longevity runs strong in our blood making death seem a distant notion, a concept we discussed with laughter and ease. Mom was in good health, performing her daily exercise routine like a religious rite. She played tournament Pickle ball and she was good at it. I used to describe it to my curious friends as kind of like playing tennis standing on a giant ping-pong table. It's a racket sport, she'd say, irritation reshaping her otherwise gentle voice. Mom was strong and active and serious about her sport, an athlete in the prime of her golden years. We all took it for granted that she would be with us well in to her nineties.

It was my birthday, my fifty-first. Living a thousand miles apart, Mom and I had always enjoyed long phone calls on our birthdays but that year we both had plans for the day and agreed to talk first thing the next morning. My plan was to spend the day slathered in self-indulgent ecstasy. A full-on pedicure, complete with Barbie Goes On A Picnic Toes—hot pink with tiny hand-painted daisies—started my day. An hour and a half long—forget the myofascial-release, please, let's focus on pure pleasure—massage followed. Next up, a trip to Salon Down Under for a hair makeover. Purple streaks, feathers in my newly coiffed bangs.

All of this was topped off with dinner at my favorite Tex-Mex restaurant, Fresh—I'm talking swimming in the sea that morning—shrimp enchiladas bellied up next to a side of praise-worthy *calabacitas* and home cooked refried black beans. Oh, did somebody say flan? I was groaning with excess.

I had always been uncomfortable with my birthday, never liked the attention. This was my big breakthrough, therapy of a sort. I thought of it as the beginning of a new era. From now on I would whoop it up just like everybody else.

The call came the next day at two thirty-seven in the afternoon. I had just begun to fret, wondering why Mom hadn't called first thing in the morning. Maybe I should call her, I'd been thinking. Maybe she had forgotten. She was seventy-eight years old after all. Maybe I should give her a break. I was in my studio working on a big silver jewelry order, the bread and butter of my financially shaky career as an artist, when the phone rang. I jumped out of my seat and grabbed for it.

The voice on the other end said, "This is Linda."

"Linda? Linda who," I said.

"Linda, your sister," the voice said.

I landed back on my chair with a thud. Something bad was coming. My sister never called me. Ever. She told me she was in the waiting room at Harborview Hospital—the regional trauma center where the worst of the worst cases go—that Mom had been in a car accident the day before, about the time all those tiny daisies were being hand-painted onto my hot pink toenails. She told me that Mom had been alone, unidentifiable, through the night because the police hadn't found her purse in the wreckage until early the next morning. She was alive, my sister said, but that her head looked like a watermelon and she was at that moment in surgery to repair multiple internal lacerations. Then she told me that our mother might die.

I live in Alaska. Mom lived in Seattle. Getting from my point A to her point B was complicated. It took me two and a half days to get to her side. When I first saw her I thought I might faint. My brother, who was now on the scene with my sister, told me that the swelling had gone down considerably though I couldn't find her face no matter how hard I tried.

We spent the next two weeks together in the ICU; my brother, my sister and I. Family dynamics were all jumbled. My brother, my big brother, was barely holding it together at times. It became my self-appointed job to make sure he ate and slept. He and I camped out at Mom's condo, heading in to the hospital early enough each morning to catch the doctors on their rounds, coming home late each evening exhausted and discouraged. Meanwhile, my sister expressed her grief and fears through random political tirades. Her rampant Republicanism brought out a feistiness in my 'old hippie' of a brother that I never knew was there. My other self-appointed job was to play referee.

Halfway through the two-week hospital stay, Mom opened her eyes, looked at each one of us. Our hopes soared. She was breathing with the help of the ventilator inserted through the slit cut in her neck. The nurses explained that the experience is so stressful the patient needs to be heavily medicated in order to bear it. They went on to say that these patients never remember any of this time, that they're not really there at all. We took turns anyhow, combing her hair, rubbing her feet, recounting old family stories. We brought in her favorite CD's hoping they might comfort her. Willie Nelson crooning, "Someone To Watch Over Me" became the theme song of our ordeal.

It wasn't their fault, those superhero/angel ICU doctors and nurses, nor due to any lack of trying, but at the end of the two weeks when nothing more could be done for her there, Mom was transferred to what is called a rehabilitation center. A place where patients on ventilators go to die. I still don't know what the stats are for sure, but if even one out of a hundred patients ever left that place alive I'd be surprised. By then the medication levels were so high Mom rarely opened her eyes. It was decided that I should go home to Alaska. My brother and sister would keep me informed as to any changes.

Back at home I couldn't stop thinking about how she wanted to go out, wrapped in a blanket of song. I took to calling her regularly, having the staff place the receiver on her pillow, singing softly to her until I heard the sharp click of disconnection when they hung up the phone after fifteen minutes or so. They told me that it was of no use, that she couldn't hear me. They only let it slip once that her near nonexistent blood pressure would rise up into the range of the living whenever I sang to her. Mostly they considered me a harmless kook from the land of igloos.

A few months later, when her last futile grasp on life became too weak to hold on any longer, I returned to Seattle to sing her out properly.

They told us to say our goodbyes then unplugged the ventilator. It might be as quick as ten minutes or as long as two hours.

Everyone was different they said, you just never knew. I began what turned out to be a three and a half day singing vigil. I left her side only for bathroom breaks, quick dashes to the cafeteria, naps in a nest of wadded up blankets on the floor of her room. After two days, my daughter joined me and they brought us a folding single bed to share. My daughter is also a singer and more than that she understood the importance of what we were doing. Folk songs, pop songs, every Sing Along With Mitch Miller song that I could dredge up from childhood memories of singing along with Mom, Mitch and the old hi-fi. From *Twinkle Twinkle* to the Beatles, everything we sang was infused with love and prayers for safe passage on her journey. Our heartfelt rendition of *Amazing Grace* drew in one of the nurses on the final night. The three of us rocked it, gospel style. I'm sure the facility had never heard anything like it. Other than my daughter's and my singing, the only sounds we ever heard there were the padding down the hallways of thick soled shoes and the shoosh shoosh shooshing of the twenty some ventilators keeping the dead alive.

I felt my mother's last breath brush my cheek as her spirit left her body behind, taking my final song of love with her. Swing low, sweet chariot, coming for to carry her home.

We all agreed to wait for Spring to scatter her ashes, when, once again the old family order went topsy-turvy. My brother and sister were at a complete loss as to the how and where of such a thing. They looked to me, the spiritual nutcase of the family. I knew the perfect place. That it would be in fact against the law, ha, minor detail. There is a wonderful freedom that goes along with being a nutcase, a lawbreaker.

Mom had grown up on Phinney Ridge, one of the older neighborhoods overlooking Seattle's beautiful Woodland Park. On my last visit with her, a month before the accident, she had been reminiscing about how much she'd loved walking through the park as a girl, then on down to Green Lake on her way to school. It was her very own wilderness she'd said.

I informed my family that we would be sprinkling Mom in the park.

"Follow me," I said with a new found confidence. "I'll know the right spot when we get there."

The whole family: siblings, spouses, grandchildren and great grandchildren were there. We meandered and marched. We skipped and somersaulted. We moved along in what must have looked like a drunken parade, winding our way through the park, the box of ashes hidden under my brother's coat, until we came upon a grove of flowering cherry trees in full blossom.

"We're here," I announced and everybody listened.

My daughter loosely herded the crowd into a circle. My son-in-law, casually and without being noticed, made his way around us smudging us with white sage. I shouted out a prayer disguised as a memory, encouraged others to do the same. We thought of it as subversive ceremony. A clear case of what they didn't know wouldn't hurt them.

There was nothing left but for the scattering of the ashes. Silence. Nobody knew the proper procedure. Again all eyes looked to me. I had no idea so I blurted out, "You just put your hand in the box, take a handful and go to it."

Silence. Not knowing what else to do I plunged my hand into the box. When my two and a half year-old granddaughter insisted on having her own handful, I couldn't see any good reason to say no so she plunged her chubby little hand in with mine and off we went in search of exactly the right depository. What choice did they have? The rest of the family soon joined in.

I can tell you now that it takes a lot more handfuls than you might think to get to the bottom of the box. By the time we were done we were all grinning through ash and tear streaked cheeks. Ashes covered our clothes, our shoes, our hands. We were happy, relived and proud. We knew that we had done right by our mother.

Someone suggested we all go out for Indian food. A general cheer arose. What a sight we must have been, as we took that restaurant by storm, some of us laughing, some of us singing, all of us eager to stuff our messy faces. It was time now for my son-in-law to take the reins. He had spent a good deal of time in India, knew the cuisine, and I was ready for someone else to be in charge. With a charming Hindi accent he ordered up a feast. None of us had any idea what we were eating. None of us cared. It was warm, delicious and plentiful. It was a celebration.

Invisible Ribbons
by Katey Lovell

The frame glistens, illuminating the darkened room.
In that frame my family is complete.
Whole.
Four beaming faces, squinting in the August sunshine.

This photograph holds my memories,
Memories of you.
The smiles we shared before the sun went to sleep.
The love we had before the winter came.

Things have changed.
You are gone.
But I still have a Dad.

We are still a family, inexplicably bound together with invisible ribbons.
Heart strings.
Family ties.

Our Hell
      by Sally K Lehman

I. Hell

By the beginning of the year we had redefined hell.
Hell is now the white condominium, one away from the golf
course, with petunias in the brick flower box by the front door.

We have to believe in this hell. Without a hell there is no heaven.
We have to have our religion of please-god-save-our-mother even
though there is no longer a god and Mom is going to die.

My sisters and I congregate at our white condo-hell and arrange
things.
Who takes care of Mom this day, the next day, three weeks from
Tuesday *if* she's still alive then? Who calls the doctor or the
hospice nurse or the ambulance *if* she needs to been seen by
someone? Who handles the paperwork and the insurance and the
will and the ashes *if* Mom dies right this very second now?

If has become our petition.
Our prayer to the godlessness we've founded.

II. Family

And as five sisters who are all adults, we must find ways to deal
with each other again.

The youngest of the sisters makes her demands on the rest of us.
She wants comfort and she wants attention and she wants
sympathy and she wants our ears and our shoulders and our ATM
Personal Identification Numbers because, all in all, what she really

wants from everyone is their money. She wants until there isn't anything left in me to give and then she wants more. She wants wants wants and I give until she has leached the last ounces of caring out of me and I just want her to go away which just makes her dissolve into poor-me tears that make me want to punch things.

My walls are in imminent danger of my fist.

The other sisters are all older than me, have been in the position to tell me what to do and me in the position to do. And not one of these three older sisters are falling into those prearranged positions I thought to expect once the words cancer and Mom were shoved together in August of the year before.

One sister was supposed to avoid all involvement.
One sister was supposed to be the step-in mother to us all.
One sister was supposed to be too busy with work to deal with life.
I was supposed to be the fount of all things medical, the one who took care of things, the voice of reason which no one else would listen to, the family messiah who is in tune with the nature of our grief and our inability to show it, because I am the one writing this and they are not.

None of us live up to my expectations.

Our avoid-it-all sister comes and sits. She brings hugs and she brings potato salad and she sits. She brings bread and she brings cookies and she sits.
> "Why does she always bring food?" another sister asks.
> "To feel like she's earned the right to be here," Mom answers.
> Mom has grown wisdom alongside her cancer.

Until the day comes when this sister brings only herself and we welcome her in and ask her to sit.

Our mother-us-all sister hides in SoCal. The white-condo-hell is too closed up airless and too real. If she can avoid the rituals of waiting for Mom to die, then Armageddon will never come and we will all be the same. Static and alive
and it doesn't work that way.
I wish sometimes I could be like her.

Our life-is-busy sister sets down her load, un-harnesses herself from a work-every-day trudge, drives ten hours north to us and takes up the new harness-trudge in Mom's blue guest bedroom. She meets with doctors and lawyers and hospice and this person and that person and fixes everything just so. She has made it possible for the rest of us to mindlessly wander the white condominium, watching every move Mom makes in case it is her last.
This is the sister who built hell.

And me.
The fourth of the five of us, the writer and reader and pompous bitch who thought only I could take on all of this illness, take on all of the chores and come gloriously out of hell with rainbows and stigmata.
I wait and watch with the rest. More useless than I have ever been before as we sacrifice our mother on the alter of in-home-hospice-care.

III. Fathers

Dad was supposed to be the bastard asshole good-for-nothing shadow of a human being that could only feel relief at the loss of his first of four wives.

Every hell needs a devil and that was the father I had built in my head.

That might have been the man Mom built in her head too, because she didn't tell him about the cancer until May of this last year of her life.

Mom wrote it in a letter mailed to the trailer park where Dad lives with wife number four. It was a heartless way to tell something and I knew bone deep that he deserved heartlessness. Vindication for lapsed child support and past drunken brawls and infidelity. Vindication that deserves the convenience of a stereotypical bad guy in the face of the world coming down around our ears.

And Dad called.

He called me and he called my sisters and he called Mom. He cried with us and asked to visit. He came to Mother's Day dinner and sat with us, the seven members of our root-rot family tree together again after a mere thirty-seven year drought.

And after Mother's Day, when he was supposed to slither off to his car and make his way west and south and away from us, he stayed. He called wife-number-four and she agreed, told him to take care of us, told him to be the man she knew him to be, told to him to stay as long as we needed him.
Wife number four has grown in my estimations.

Dad now sits with us, waits with us, watches Mom.
He administrates pain medicines and walks to the 7-11 to buy Mom cigarettes.

They joke about their youth while Mom makes the foods she made so very long ago – fried chicken and baking soda biscuits and chicken gravy and green beans. We talk about mundane things while we eat.

And questions build
>   Could they have ever been this normal kind of couple?
>   What would it have been like to grow up with them like this?
>   Is this how everyone else spent childhood?

My parents have built me a purgatory of *What ifs*.

IV. Me

I wish sometimes that I was an alcoholic. A constant, medically recognized drunkenness would be nice.

Or maybe I wish I was a better liar. That I could look my daughters in the eye, look my husband in the eye, and say that I am fine and everything is fine and we will get through this unscathed and sane and fine.

I want to hide behind my mother's legs.
I want to hide behind the doors and the curtains and the walls of my house.
I want to hide in my room, head under the covers, door locked until someone has to take it off the hinges just to get in.
I want to live there, die there, wait there on the feather pillowed comfortable rectangle of my bed.
I wait for the knocking sounds of someone needing me.
I want to answer the knocking with "There's no one in here" because I am empty of me so it's true.

I cannot let them in, my husband, my daughters, because I will contaminate them with my loss and my sorrow and the hole where my heart is supposed to still be.

I am broken, and do not want to break them.

V. Hell

In hell, Mom doesn't eat anymore. Cancer has blocked the path from her stomach to the rest of her body. She makes dinner and watches us eat.

In hell, Mom's pelvic bones stand out in vertical mountain peaks. She only wears sweat pants because anything without an elastic waist falls off.

In hell, someone always has to be with Mom when she takes the stairs, someone must be willing to catch her if she falls so she doesn't break.

In hell, we wait until we no longer have to.

Worm
        by Jessica Standifird

I want to worm my way into Mom's dysfunction,
feed on any similarities her passing has left behind.

The soil is old but moist, full of possibility--
disease or growth given the circumstance.

You tunnel to her core, Dad.
Blind, thumbless,
you build a home in her belly and ingest the leftover rot.

We are slick with tears and ignorance;
without their protective coat we shrivel to nothing.

We churn beneath her skin,
stitch pockets of oxygen into shriveled lungs.
Each segment pushes the next one forward.

When we find the surface we wrap around each other
to form a tangled, confused fist.

Our twenty hearts beat like the rhythm of her voice
as it calls us home for supper.

Hit Or Miss
        by Jessica Standifird

We were always hit or miss,
Dad and daughter.
Sometimes we would talk for hours.
Laughter filled our mouths as quickly
as your whiskey glass emptied.
Other times, it was just plain awkward.

I lift you into the passenger side of your truck
and take my turn in the driver's seat.
Yeah, this is going to be one of those awkward times.
It's going to be rough.

I want to put your cowboy hat
on top of the box that holds your ashes
but I'm not quite quirky enough to pull it off
with the flair I'd like to.

I want to be strong enough to talk to you
as I drive us home,
to make wisecracks and reminisce.

Instead I stare straight ahead,
ignore the coffee stains in the cup holders,
fight the stale smoke blasting
from the dusty vents

and hope that for once you were wrong
and you are

somewhere other

than ash.

Cheap Wrapping Paper in a Cardboard Coffin
by Sean Davis

A Mexican woman I didn't know called to tell me she found my father dead and naked on her living room floor.

When I was a kid, especially an adolescent, I blamed Dad for how poor we were, I blamed him for how all the other kids would make fun of us growing up in our trailer park, and I blamed him for all the faults I found in myself. I'd say that if I just had a regular father and a regular family like the other children, my social skills and ability to form relationships wouldn't have been handicapped. If he would have spent some time with me maybe I'd have a fully formed sense of worth and some self-confidence. If he would have just given a damn about being a father my life would have been easier.

I have a son and two daughters and I have to watch it because if I stare at any of them for too long it brings me to tears. I love them that much. A big man like me brought to tears. It happens more than I'll admit and in those times I can't see how anyone wouldn't love their children and do anything for them. So I've spent hours, days, probably weeks trying to figure out Dad.

My father was a product of the Me Generation and while I think the 70s were a great time to be born it proved a very bad time for a nineteen year old kid to become a parent. He was young, living in San Francisco during a decade full of all types of brand new drugs. Alcoholism was almost a rite of passage and narcissism was the zeitgeist. My parents fumbled at marriage long enough to have two more sons. Then both of them let the drinking and drugs get out of control. Luckily, both sets of my grandparents had lived through depressions, world wars, and national tragedies so three parentless grandchildren were not a huge challenge.

Dad left when I was five. My brothers were three and one. We didn't see him again until he drunkenly crashed through the front door of his parent's single-wide trailer years later. My grandparents saw us growing and realized they were too old to raise teenagers again. They called Dad and he came. He was in his own suspended adolescence from the drugs and alcoholism, he didn't have the ability or disposition to parent children, but he came. Does he get points for that? Does he get points for going out and marrying the first woman he could find that would be okay with staying at home with his three boys while he blistered his hands and feet working a chainsaw in the wet forests of the Cascade Mountains? I would like to give him some, but he was an abusive drunk. My brothers and I would go to school on several occasions with black eyes, swells, and bruises and had to make up stories about how we got them.

I left home at fifteen and by sixteen lived on my own. For years I'd go to high school all day and work as a night stocker at our local supermarket. A few years after graduating I joined the military and in that time I was deployed to a revolution, a war, and a few natural disasters and I know I saved lives in all of these places. Does Dad get points for giving me drive, independence, or discipline? Does he get points for creating a life where I saw no other option than joining the military? How much credit does he get for those people I saved? I don't know, but I do know Dad tried, not his hardest, but he tried.

I had visited him a few months before he died and at that time he was still with the woman he married to raise my brothers and me, but he shared secret plans to leave her for his Mexican girlfriend. His new drug of choice came from hospitals in little orange bottles. He didn't care what they're names were or their intended purpose. He'd throw a bunch down his throat just to see what they'd do. I wanted my wife to meet him before he was gone. I can't say why.

The night I found out he died I called my brothers. The next day we drove the length of Oregon and most of California to Woodlawn Memorial Cemetery. After telling the lady at the front desk who we were, a man in a nice suit was called. This man blushed when he explained to us that no one had come to sign papers, visit the deceased, or bring clothes. Dad had been brought straight there so when he opened the door to the dark cremation room there was Dad, completely naked inside of "the most cost effective" coffin they had, which was made of thick cardboard. In order to preserve the decease's dignity, the man told me, they had covered his lower body with a translucent plastic "blanket".

When I saw him I couldn't help but to burst out laughing. My brother Vince asked with a smile if we were going to mail him somewhere. Keith just stared down at Dad's face. Trying to recover I kept my eyes on him for a few seconds but the way the muscles had relaxed, I didn't really even see the dad I knew, so I looked away.

The man blushed deeper and awkwardly informed us that he was going to leave us to grieve. He said he'd be back and asked us how much time we would need. I asked him what would be appropriate. He coughed and said he'd be back in ten or fifteen minutes.

My brothers and I looked at each other not knowing what to do. My children never knew Dad except for in a couple faded pictures. In the twenty years of my adulthood I'd gotten to know him better and despite all his faults he was my father. I'd call him at least a few times a month and he'd be sober maybe half the time. Sometimes he would speak to my kids and every once in a while he would send them something for the holidays. A few desperate times he sent me money and came through when I really needed help. Maybe it was important to acknowledge he wasn't a total asshole now that he was covered in cheap wrapping paper in a cardboard coffin.

When the man came back, a guy with his thick black hair slicked back, a handlebar mustache and a neck tattoo of a Mexican sugar skull was with him to complete the cremation process. The name on his greased stained jumpsuit said Jesus. Dad was never a religious man that I knew about, but if he had been this was the Jesus he would have wanted. This was the Jesus he deserved.

My Mother As Tree
  by Claudia Savage

   Sitting beside her, my hands are sun.
The frost that's taken her hair and skin thaws.
     Lifting her chin,

I am daffodils.

My sister's weeping, my father's mouthing *terminal* like a pierced balloon
mean nothing. This is our moment. Desire is a swifter river than death.

I'll dream the blood in her legs mountain runoff.
Leaning forehead to forehead, the words *mother, please*

  set her heart once more a thunder.

One Final Indignity
    by Rick Blum

We gathered in the mid-morning calm of this artificial oasis before the heat would drive us into air-conditioned cocoons to share fading family memories.

We had traveled from a half dozen corners of the lower 48 to bid farewell to the tough, old crow who lived life out loud, in fullness – now uncharacteristically silent as four leather-faced vets inched slowly toward the flag-draped casket. She had earned this ceremonial military send-off by being among the first to join the Women's Army Corps when Hitler was rampaging across Europe and women were considered too delicate for war.

After the one-time warriors had solemnly stationed themselves behind the raised coffer, she listened helplessly as their wizened spokesman intoned, "Shirley served America in its greatest time of need. *He* was a true patriot."

Thus, the woman who worked tirelessly to support her family while her husband went to medical school, who earned her own degree at night 15 years later, who trekked across the far corners of America, Europe, China and the Middle East, was unwittingly reduced to an unexceptional *he*.

And desperately needing a champion on that final day in the company of the living, her progeny froze in place as the discordant pronoun washed over the bereaved, speaking not a word in the faint hope that this would be a singular mistake.

It was not.

Later, while noshing on deli and rich desserts, they tried to laugh off this one final indignity as somehow an ironic ending to a feisty woman's journey. But behind the smiles, we could all hear her voice defiantly calling out in the dry desert air, "I'm a *she*, dammit!"

I Can't Remember the Sound of My Father's Voice
by Fern G Z Carr

I search for the sound
of my father's voice
in the ether of memory –
snippets,
remnants,
anything….

princess bedtime stories,
cheering at hockey games on tv,
refereeing sibling battles,
chats in the car
en route to piano lessons

and a deathbed request
to never let my mother
walk the dog
alone
at night.

I remember the things
my father said
but I can't remember
the sound of his voice
and the harder I try
the more difficult it becomes.

Now That You're Dead
by Fern G Z Carr

Dad, now that you're dead,
your atoms a mess of entropy,
s-p-r-a-y-e-d
across a universe
of recycled
matter and energy,

do you look down
omniscient,
omnipresent,
to eavesdrop
on friends and relatives
who badmouth you
and sing your praises?

Do you judge?
Do you communicate?
Can you?

Are you telepathic?
Do you have superpowers

or are you nothing now
but a hunk of
maggot chow?

Hard to Believe
by Fern G Z Carr

hard to believe
that that's that
fini
nada

hard to believe
that all that's
   left
are teeth   bones
and possibly
jewelry

What Happened On My Eighteenth Birthday
by Adam Loewen

The main thing I remember about that day is the sun. It really seemed to be taking up too much of the sky, splashing into places where it didn't belong, reflecting everything back into me. I was genuinely concerned that the world was ending. Not just my world, my little situation, but everyone. The sun was exploding. For me, there really wasn't much difference. I figured, "Hey, if the world's got to end while I'm around, might as well be right now, this moment."

As far as I know, there was nothing going on with the sun. It was still winter, technically, though no longer so harsh that you couldn't walk around comfortably outside. Missoula, snow covered the ground all through January. Crunch, crunch, crunch. I walked along the river path, just because I had nowhere to go, nothing to get away from, no reason to move at all and no reason not to.

My body crunched over the packed crust of ice. The river made a soft commotion underneath its winter cover, and light filled up the sky like those blobs inside a lava lamp, but I couldn't tell what its color was. Blue, red, yellow, no color, all color, black, it was oppressive, and I was numb all over.

I walked this trail often. It best maximized beauty per distance from my front door, and it was somewhat private. Whatever I was going to feel, I would allow it.

I was not crying yet. Hadn't found my *in*, I guess. I wasn't really thinking about anything, not really *feeling* anything, but my intestines grumbled at odd intervals and I knew on some level that I was doing little more than allowing the weight of this to catch up with me. I thought, maybe it never *will* catch up. Maybe this is how I take things.

I felt nothing. Was I okay? That's what everyone was going to ask me for the rest of my life. I shouldn't have been, but what they wouldn't understand is that I was. Everything was okay. This is how things are. If you don't know that people die, you're the one that's not okay.

What am I missing here? I thought to myself. It felt like a part of me was gone. Not like that; I mean, it felt like part of my brain had shut down. This was certainly an altered state of consciousness.

The night before didn't feel like a thousand years ago. It felt like the night before. I had gone to Finnegann's "family restaurant" around midnight, with Jim and Bob, probably Johann. We stayed there, like we always did, until around 2am. That's when the bar rush came in, and the whole vibe just changed.

Around midnight, it was all about the stoned, young intellectuals and tabletop gaming nerds. This girl, Lindsey, came into the restaurant, and she and her friend even came and sat with us boys. I could tell Lindsey had some sort of crush on me, curiosity at least. It was not common for girls to be interested in me. I was seventeen years old and never had a girlfriend.

Actually, that was the night I turned eighteen. I made no show of it. I've always hated my birthday. Even back then.

I'll never really know what happened to my mom that night. I woke up the following morning, probably about noon, with three dudes crashed around my big converted garage bedroom. I grabbed some shorts and a tee shirt and headed upstairs to shower. There was a spring in my step. I guess it was because of Lindsey, but I wasn't really aware of that. I sang to myself in the shower, which wasn't exactly ordinary for me. I came out of the bathroom, kind of in a hurry to get past the living room before grandma interrogated me about whatever was worrying her in those particular days.

"Honey?"

Too late. I was captured. Grandma was sitting in her chair, permanently settled into a contour the shape of her back and bottom, like a sweet, adorable version of Emperor Palpatine. Sitting across from her in a wooden chair was a man I'd never seen before. I assumed he was one of grandma's old traveling friends. They do this. Old people. They have all these friends littered from all different parts of their life, and these people come by to visit once every decade or so. There's enough of them that we were seeing maybe one every two weeks. It was always awkward and boring for me, so I was careful to dodge those situations.

This man was typical. Mustache, glasses, rosy cheeks. He was a sheriff, too, apparently. Kind of weird to wear his uniform in here to visit grandma.

"Honey, could you come in here and sit down for a second?" grandma said, and she sounded normal. A little grave, but not losing her shit. Not hysterical. It's a family trait. Or maybe this is just how people are. But in the movies, people are hysterical when stuff like this happens.

"We've got some bad news."

The sheriff speaks to me, slowly. I grow increasingly uncomfortable. Yes, I get it. Should I cry? Should I scream and run or something? I just stood there, kind of half grinning. I knew he didn't think I understood what he was saying, but I absolutely did. And I thought, "God dammit, mom. I knew something like this would happen."

We all did.

I had nothing to say to the sheriff. He told me everything I'd want to know. No foul play. No suicide. It wasn't really an accident, even. Just one of those things, that happens.

"Thank you," I said to the sheriff.

Mom had been living in a bus that year, outside of town. Before that, she always lived in this house, under grandma's wing, taking care of us kids. Dad existed, there were boyfriends, but from my perspective it was always just mom and boys. Mom and me, really, and some of my friends, because Laramie and Kiam had never really been nest babies. My entire life, mom had devoted herself to me.

Here I was, though, full grown. I guess it was about time for her to let go of it all and find her own way. She had no money, not much going on other than an antique refinishing business and a charming personality that she herself underrated way too much.

She moved into a school bus with bales of hay packed under it for insulation, consorting with these homeless stoner types. Down by the river.

And I wasn't mad at her, I didn't judge her. I came out to the bus and we talked about life, and she smoked me up, and we got little inflatable things and floated on the river with the two dogs, Byron and Ken-Dog, running all around barking.

She wasn't an alcoholic, but she was depressed. Every now and then, she drank too much and then she would want to drive or vandalize some property that belonged to one of dad's girlfriends. Things like that.

One time, I had to duct tape her hands and legs together to prevent her from driving the truck to the store to get cigarettes, because she was too drunk. I had her trapped in the bathroom, and she hopped toward me, pathetically, angry but laughing. But then she fell, and her head hit the linoleum and I knew it would leave a bruise, and she couldn't stop herself from falling all taped together. She looked up at me as she fell, then on her knees, drunk and stupid, in the bathroom, she just burst out crying. And it melted me. So, I immediately ripped off all the tape, and she charged out the front door, slammed it, and went and got her cigarettes.

It's not like she or I knew she would die, but we both knew it was a possibility, an eventuality. I didn't hold it against her. If she died, I would still be there for her.

And so, here I was crunching along with her, leaving footprints in the snow, because she had become the sun and she was more fierce and passionate than anything her little boy could ever dream up. I was still just crunch, crunch, crunching down here. She had ascended. And she left me here. But she was still here. I had more snow-crunching to do, and in between, I would have these dreams...

Oh, there you are. Of course you're not really dead, but mom, seriously, where have you been all these years?

Would you believe it? I really thought you were dead. Oh, that's just so funny.

And then there's that dissonance in the dream, where you know it's a dream, but it's still real. This isn't really my mom, but she's around here somewhere. What kind of nonsense are you talking? How could she be dead? I *know* her. She has this habit of driving around with an empty gas tank, and the fuel light is just the first of many indicators that it's time to drop another five in the tank if you can possibly manage it.

In spite of this, she came to see me on my birthday. We never spent this much time apart before. She was getting sentimental with me. Just weeks before, she came to the house to see me in the late afternoon. She didn't seem drunk, but there was something a little off about her. Like maybe she was afraid, but she didn't want me to know. She stood by the side of my bed for a long time. I was sleeping out on the deck, basically a roof and some chicken wire and wood separating me from the elements. I liked the smell of real air when I went to bed, and to hear the animals and traffic and neighborhood kids around me in the night made it easier to sleep.

I woke up and saw her, and she smiled the warmest smile I've ever seen. "I love you, sweetheart," she said. I looked down and saw that her elbow was injured. She didn't remember how these things kept happening. The elbow was gnarly. It was the kind of tear you'd get from a bicycle crash, but she had probably just fallen over. It needed stitches. She wasn't going to go to a doctor. It would leave a scar. She would have many scars, just building and building until her beautiful face and youthful body had all the character of a genuine, "salt of the Earth" sort of antique.

I didn't even ask about the bloody composite flesh on her elbow. She held my hand for a moment, then sat on the bed, fell back and cuddled with me. I was crying, but my face was hidden. I really missed her. Grandma came in and snapped a picture, said hi to mom, and then left before any arguing could occur.

I never saw her on my eighteenth birthday. She came to the house while I was at Finnegann's. She had brought some friend of hers, some Native American guy I had met once or twice. I'm not sure if there was a romantic thing between them. Maybe he wanted to, as many of those guys did. The only thing he and I had in common was a love for the peach moonshine he brewed up in big mason jars with plastic bags rubberbanded over the lid.

She and this guy and the two dogs came to the house in the pickup truck, like a drunken circus. Grandma told them I wasn't home, so they eventually decided to go back to the bus without me. It was about forty miles from my house. They ran out of gas. They marched through snow to the closest bar, and at some point, mom flipped out, apparently.

This was a side of her that came out every now and then. She became completely outraged and inconsolable, and in that state, she tended to abandon people, scream, and slam doors. She raged out at the bar by the side of the snowy road just before Clearwater Junction. It was mostly dark, but moonlight reflected between the snow and clouds. Probably at or below freezing. Who knows what was going through her head.

She never made it back to the truck. The Native guy left the bar without ever tracking her down. I never saw him again, but he was the one that ended up taking the dogs. Her body was found a little ways off from the side of the road early in the morning by a man just going about his business. Her clothing had gotten soaked, she had gotten hypothermia, and she just collapsed in the snow and slept.

After talking with the sheriff, I walked back down into the converted garage that was my bedroom. Jim, Bob, and Johann were all awake, sluggish. They knew something was up.

"Guys?" I said. "Mom's dead."

There was no change in anything. Three sluggish boys, rubbing their eyes, one with wet hair standing in the middle of the room.

"She's dead, guys," I repeated. "Josephine fucking died. Froze to death." I didn't say it any particular way. They didn't react any particular way. We all understood. We were not in denial. Mom was dead. *Our* mom was dead. There was nothing else to say.

Eventually, I would have to play my part in the next stage of everything. I would have to drive up Pattee Canyon and tell Laramie, and I'd have to make all sorts of phone calls. Everyone would bring me gifts and thoughts, sit in the corner of the room awkwardly with nothing to say. They were afraid to say anything nice or funny for the next six months, because they didn't want to make me feel uncomfortable. Everyone knew I was closer to mom than anyone else in the world. They would give me space and time to deal with it, but their perspective of me had changed. I was, in some way, supposed to become the new Josephine, because everybody knew she had invested everything into me.

My friends had already made plans for the day. I was still entertaining the notion of participating, but I knew that eventually, this thing was going to hit me. It just hadn't yet. So, I just left the house, to take a walk. I was just walking, through the snow, feeling my mother's soul bleed into every shadow of my reality as clear, penetrating light, and the sun, and God, and Josephine, and the universe, squeezing me like a sponge until finally the tears came.

I talked to her, to the sun. Crunching, sobbing, I thought she was more beautiful than ever. People who knew Josephine, they'll tell you the truth. She was always the sun. Not just because she was my mom, not because she was dead, there was just something about her. She was special. She never really belonged in this world.

I would spend the rest of my life making her proud, even though she'd never see it, and even though she'd be proud no matter what. I asked her one time what she thought was the hardest thing in the world, and she said that it must be songwriting.

The first song I ever wrote was about her, but I never play it.

Pedestrian Visions
by Judith Pullman

Whether entering or packing to leave,
Dream-mother's ceaselessly in motion
Like a young girl's spinning top
That gushes colors till it collapses.

Then, she ceases all motion
As her slender ankles bulge and her lips
Gush colors. She collapses
With a sudden pang. She is dead now;

Her ankles bulging, her lips
Thinned. It's afternoon. Rain repeats,
Pang after pang, *She's dead,*
Remember? The heart's walls are too

Thin. Afternoon rain repeats.
She explained the roots of her disease,
Remember: the walls of her heart were
Wrenched. You salt your wound

By explaining the roots of your dis-ease,
How you feel without her:
Wrenched, assaulted, and wounded
Since she wouldn't stay.

How do you feel without her?
Unkempt, naughty. You wish you could pause more
But know that you can't stay.
To value bloody spirits means to heed

These knotty feelings, like the wish to pause more
Or to be a young girl. Stop:
Why value long-gone blood? Save spirit, take heed.
Every time you enter, she packs up to leave.

Last Words
by Judith Pullman

Suddenly it's your turn to give a eulogy.
To let the crowd know that death has been trapped
In this sad case, this pine box. They need you,
For you have caught something special.

Thank you is the only proper response.

Making sense of life is hard, but making
Sense of *a* life feels dumb. The last word?
Nope. Just the first where the dead don't
Get to amend your wobbly speech.

This is when a collective recollection
Adds up to a missing whole
That sticks around, true or not. After the change
Posterity hangs, a bauble on a bulky chain.

Though then again the dead, they don't quite cohere;
They'd fall apart reciting their story
If they were to come back. Choking on tears
They'd die a second death, a sight to make

Even the sickos break down in anguish.

So buck up and trace that graveside arc,
The somber procession craves a word that lasts
And a simple gesture dividing present from past—
You are everything the dead had hoped

After Frost, Leaving the Yellow Woods
by Judith Pullman

Two parents went to flesh on winter eves.
I was sorry that I had outlived both
And was just one child, so I tried to grieve
And root in their soil for eternities,
And die too, amidst some undergrowth.

My friends stood off awhile, giving me room
As I clawed at those graves—*come back, come back!*
Some had lost one parent, none had lost two,
And though father was a sometime name, which I knew,
I wept, since I sought to have and not lack.

My mother's flesh had much longer lain
In that damp earth, below the broad stone.
A rose branch was carved around her name
And some words about music and love, the same
That seemed true before, now felt overblown.

The path led uphill, past both their plots,
And my mouth wanted food and was desperate to talk.
The soul's its own animal, it would rather move than not:
My parents had gone so I began my slow trot
Away, and I have so much further to walk.

Figuring Absence
by Judith Pullman

Maybe you should write it *ab-sense*,
Some lack of presence that you bump
Against; itinerant lint that clings
To your pillow and gets on your face.

Did you notice the missing half
And half? Was it you who had it yesterday?
You drink your inky coffee slow and think
How you always had a taste for bitterness.

You get that the them that was there now isn't
But the furniture doesn't seem to forget.
The sofa keeps keening; you sell it, let it go,
And blue shall have no dominion.

You resolve to *live* in your living room.
As you lie down to sleep, dust rises up,
Infecting your eyes. You shake
Your rag at the querulous air,

How can you sleep when nothing is there?

post holes
     by Francis X. LaChapelle

if you grew up on a farm you know how to dig a hole . gloves wear
through fighting dirt with a

spade and a maul for the iron bar to bust up boulders . holes have
to go where the post must

be so rocks are broken . the small brother holds the bar wincing
and hoping for the clang of

metal at the long end of the swing . sitting with mom and her
third fracture as the specialist

tells where he will drive the pins to fix it this time but I don't hear
beyond her letting go .

outside the window in the garden water smoothes the stone and
ferns fall like her fingers over

my calluses . and it strikes me my brothers and I in that pasture
were doctors too building

this fence breaking bones and flesh .

Do it Right The First Time
by Madeline Beckwith

Three painstakingly neat ponytails on all three daughters
the only hair style you had mastered for expedience and order
your military training taught you to fold each towel the same way
before stacking them in neat perfectly even rows in the linen closet
so that you would not pull the top towel from a pile
and watch the whole stack topple
do it right the first time ... was your motto
but that never worked with children
the three of us stood stock still before you in white panties and tank
tops
you sighed as your eyes came to rest on me
my left ponytail slightly askew and my white tube socks slouching
impudently toward my ankles
as though my entire being resisted straightening and stacking

  a harbinger of things to come

you resigned yourself to constantly straightening my ponytail, pulling
up my tube socks and double tying my tennis shoes
do it right the first time ... was your motto
but that never worked with children
or as you would find out later... with women

You would relay messages through my sisters
because my tears disarmed you
You did not know how to fight someone who fought with tears
instead of fist
we never understood each other,
You thought my weekly poetry slam was a cult
I thought the church you presided over was a tax exempt gang
but love seeps through cracks and openings of similarities
unacknowledged

and we would later find out that we are both susceptible to infections
do it right the first time ... was your motto
But that never worked...
we shared a coma for two days through
2293 miles from Omaha to Las Vegas...
I dreamed of you
You with Valley Fever me with necrotizing fasciitis
I dreamed of you driving me around in a car
because that is the only place we truly connected driving me to high school forensics competitions...
college campus journalism meetings...
and, yes, even poetry slams
telling me I should get a teaching certificate
instead of a journalism degree
and me defying you and working in a call center...
Deciding you were right about that teaching certificate...

So now I struggle to go back to college and maybe this time I'll get that teaching degree
but probably not...
do it right the first time ... was your motto
but that never worked with children
or as you would find out later... with women

        ... and least of all with me.

Don't Leave Me
    by Madeline Beckwith

And this is how the mind breaks
Scattered memories of you and me
We are driving around in your old Monte Carlo
I haven't seen since I was eight
we never seem to get anywhere
we talk of really nothing
the way we always did
but it is interspersed with great bits of truth
the way it always was

We are driving through a vacant parking lot and I see one of your
friends getting into a car with a young girl in a trashy outfit.
I know his wife and I love her.

She has nursed my hurts and fed my lonely when my own mother
was drinking away her own bad childhood.

I ask, "Daddy, please slow down,?" but you refuse.
You tell me not to get involved.
But, I tell you, "I am going to call her," but you stay my hand and
hold it tight.
You say to me,

    "Baby, it's always the women who suffer."

I slowly surface to reality of tubes and beeps and IVs and the
nurse
Your face morphs into the nurses face a soft pink and grey halo
surrounding her body.

    "It's always the women who suffer."

The halo slowly shifts to only pink as her words align themselves in my mind, "Are you okay?"
My eyes adjust only long enough to find an empty chair. "No, I'm not okay."
I remember the phone and I remember dialing your number
You had left my side for less than an hour.
To shower - to sleep
You had done neither
But you came anyway
When you arrived you stared down at my sleeping form
You told me,

"Comas are boring."

He was in My Dream Again Last Night
by Madeline Beckwith

I don't cry at his bedside
touch his hand and try to warm it through rubber gloves
Every surface of my body is covered in paper or latex
To protect him from me or to protect me from him
But it only seems to stop the humanity from bleeding through
I remove my mask to kiss his forehead
because I know it is the last time

...

I cry silently in the hospital hallway
the expressions on the faces of passers bear more panic than
sympathy
Their eyes plead with me to keep my grieving confined to his
room
They know there's no pathogen in this hospital more contagious
than tears
– I force swallow the golf ball lodged in my throat –
– Square my shoulders – clean my face –
and return to his bedside armored but disarmed –
Because I don't want him to remember me like that
His baby girl broken down and begging for his strength
I want him to be comforted that I will be alright
Although, I won't

...

At the airport I breathe out regret and inhale sorrow
In a labored steady rhythm
Coating my lungs with pain and unshed tears
And I don't know if I can take another breath

...

So I whisper songs like prayers
And I realize that he has never heard me sing
And I wish that there was still time to show him the closest thing
I've got to graceful
The closest that I get to grace
But I know I will not see him again until the funeral

...

I have no physical possessions to remember him by
Like time they have been stolen from me by chance and
circumstance
And like his recipe for savory cornbread, I will never get them
back
What I have left of him I carry through this airport
Baggage I cannot check or stow or unpack

...

An egg allergy– a childhood love of white bread – a shared hatred
of dark meat chicken – an ever a maturing love of all things
legume – a genetic predisposition towards bunions – a hairy
forehead
and the trace of his crooked teeth in the smile in my mirror ...
Will have to be enough

...

I always bemoan the fact that I got all of his bad qualities and
none of his good
But, I hope the things that were so very good in him
are buried deep beneath the surface of my heart like a seed
that will some day take root

...

He was in my dream again last night
He was wearing his Dallas Cowboys hat and smiling
I will never know
if this was his goodbye, a plea for help, or just to keep me
company
He did say he was fine and that my boyfriend and I could keep his
room
But he was always saying things like that.

Bye Bye Daddy
    by Susan Pierce

By the time we had arrived at the hospital, word got out that I was taking the boys to see their father for the last time. The chief of police gave all the officers time off for the occasion. The boys, only four years old, were dressed in matching Hayward Police Officer t-shirts. Shirts their daddy had brought home from work only a few weeks before.

"We finally get to wear them," Joey said, not knowing why he and his twin were able to wear them that day.

When we turned the corner toward the intensive care wing, the entire length of the hallway was lined with officers all dressed in uniform. Stoic, strong and teary-eyed. Billy sucked in his breath and leaned in closer to me.

"Are they all here to see Daddy?" Joey asked.

"Yes, baby. They're here for Daddy and for us."

A hush fell as we walked the length of the corridor. The officer's tried not to make eye contact, yet Joey couldn't help but smile and wave to the friends we knew. Some waved back. Other's stared straight ahead doing their best to keep it together.

I pressed the button to enter the ICU. The nurse buzzed us in and met us at the double doors. The boys grew uncharacteristically quiet and gripped each of my hands a little tighter. They looked up at me, chubby cheeked and fresh faced, brown eyes wide with innocence. "Where's Daddy?" they said in unison.

"This way," I led them toward his private room, the hospital bed lowered so four-year-old faces could see onto it. Another nurse quickly closed the door when we entered.

"Wow!" Joey yelled and ran into the room. "Daddy's got his own TV. And look at the view, Mommy, come look. Look at all those houses. We're so high up. How high up are we, Mommy?" He yanked on my arm to drag me toward the window. At Joey's insistent pulling, I let go of Billy's hand.

Billy stopped cold in his tracks. He pressed his body back against the door and stared at his father lying in the bed. Tubes and cords were taped to his chest and connected to monitors beeping with each slow beat of his heart, hissing with each shallow breath. A white bandage wrapped around his head partially covered the staples above his ear where they'd done emergency brain surgery to reduce the swelling. Dried blood peaked out of his nostrils and the wound at his temple.

"That's not my dad," he whispered. "Those aren't his feet."

I glanced in the direction he was staring and noticed what he must have seen. The paleness. The stillness. "It is your Daddy, honey. But he does look different."

"No," Billy shook his head. "That's not my Daddy. That man's dead."

"Mom, look! Daddy even has his own pitcher of water and cups." Joey touched item after item on the bed tray, completely ignorant of his brother's feelings or the fact that his dad lay near lifeless in the bed. I let go of Joey's hand and went to his brother.

"Billy," I bent down to be eye level with him. "He's not dead, but you're right. He is dying. This will be the last time you get to see your daddy. Do you want to go up to him and say goodbye?"

Billy shook his head. I tried to gently coax him to his father's side with a little nudge forward, but he shook his head more vehemently.

"Mommy?" Joey stood by his father now. "When is Daddy going to wake up?"

Fuck. This was too much. My heart wanted to burst then and there. I wanted to fall down and scream but knew that I couldn't. How I reacted right then in that exact moment was something that the boys would remember forever. If I wasn't strong for them through this, then what chance would they have to be emotionally strong in the years to come?

"Joey, come here, honey." I took his little hand in mine with Billy's. "Boys. Do you remember how I told you Daddy was riding his motorcycle to work and a deer jumped out and they both accidentally ran into each other?"

"Yes," they said in unison.

"Well, that hurt your daddy really bad. It hurt his head. And the doctors, they have tried everything they can but it's not enough to make him better." As I said the words, my throat wanted to close down, I wanted to cry and rage and curl up into the bed with my husband forever, but I couldn't do any of that. "So Daddy is not going to wake up," I said.

"Ever?' Joey asked.

"Ever," I stated as matter-of-factly as I could so they wouldn't question the severity.

"I'm sorry." I bit the inside of my cheek to deflect the pain tearing my heart and stabbing theirs. "He's dying. This is the very last time you will see him. Please tell him you love

him. Tell him what a great daddy he was. Give him a kiss." My voice became pleading. "Please, boys. This is your last time and I know it would mean so much to him."

Joey's eyes began to water. He ran toward the bed and flung himself at his dad. He wrapped his arms around his father's muscled arm and pressed his face against his skin.

"No, Daddy, don't die. You can't die. No, Daddy. I don't want you to die."

Billy didn't move. He watched Joey with his dad but he didn't cry. He didn't react at all. After a moment he looked toward me and said, "Can I leave?"

Would he be sorry later if I let him go? Would it traumatize him if I made him stay? I glanced at the nurse who had done such a wonderful job cleaning up the room for the boys' arrival and for being a confidante to me throughout these painful days. She nodded. And so I did what I thought was best for Billy. "Yes, Sweetheart. Let Joey have another moment and then we can go."

He waited in silence, his big round eyes looking as old as mine.

"Joey, babe." I grasped his shoulders and hugged him. "Give Daddy a kiss and say goodbye."

"Will it hurt him?" he asked, choking back a sob.

"No, honey. Nothing can hurt him now. In fact, it would make him so happy."

"How do you know, Mommy?"

"Oh, I know."

Joey leaned over and kissed his dad's forehead. "Goodbye, Daddy. I will love you in my heart forever."

I guided them out of the room and into a private area set aside for the family. The chief of police waited. A grief counselor sat next to her. When the boys walked in the counselor offered them blank paper and crayons. "Would you like to draw what you're feeling right now?" she said with a trained tenderness.

Joey wiped his face with the back of his hands. "Yes," he brightened. "Can I draw my daddy a picture? Can we put it in his room? Next to the TV, where he can see it?"

Billy tugged on my arm. "Mom, can we go back to Daddy's room?"

Puzzled, I knelt down thinking there was no way this old soul was four and not forty. "I thought you didn't want to be in there."

"I want to go back. Please."

"Ok, sure sweetheart. Let's go." I left Joey in the care of the counselor.

We slipped back into the room, this time without any nurses. Billy walked straight up to the hospital bed and stared at his dad. Their faces at the same height.

"Bye bye, Daddy. You're the best Daddy in the whole world."

"Do you want to give him a kiss?" I asked.

"No. I'm done. I just didn't want him to think I didn't want to say goodbye."

I nodded. "That's good, Billy. It's important. Daddy's body will be gone but he'll live forever in your heart. Forever. Do you know that? That's where his spirit goes."

"Yeah." He nodded as if he already knew it and didn't need my words of assurance. "Can we go now?"

"Absolutely." I guided him out.

That night my husband died. I knew, like the nurses knew, that he'd been hanging on to see the boys one last time. In the silence of the room that night, alone, I stood by his bed.

"It's all up to me now, huh?" I said, sad, angry, and exhausted. This had not been part of our agreement. We had promised that no matter what, we would stay together, tough it out for the sake of the boys' well-being. I had counted on that promise.

His strong facial features seemed almost to soften in the dim light of the hospital room. I imagined he was saying, "I'm sorry."

The funeral was a huge production. He was not only a fallen officer, but also a long-time baseball player. Twelve hundred people turned out for the service. The boys, dressed in slacks, vests and ties, rode in the truck of the processional. Over and over people complimented the boys on how handsome they looked. How much like his daddy Billy looked.

Every day thereafter, Billy wore the suit. I'd wash it at night, hang it to dry and then on again it would go, including the tie, even if he was running out to play soccer.

About three weeks after the service I woke in the middle of the night to Billy standing by my bed staring at me. "Hey, Mom," he said when my eyes fluttered open and I was able to focus on him.

"Hey, Billy. What's up?"

"I was wondering who was going to get money to feed us?" His expression looked too serious for a child, too rigid until he blinked and in the depths of his childish eyes I saw the anxiety.

"I will, Sweetheart. You don't have to worry about that. I'll take care of us now."

"Oh, well. Daddy always did it."

"Yes, you're right." I picked my head up from the pillow so he could see I was serious. "You don't have to worry, honey. Mommy will take care of us."

"Ok." He turned, then stopped and turned back. "Who's going to take us to Disneyland?"

"I'll do that, too."

"Ok, goodnight." He kissed my cheek and then whispered, "I think Joey peed his bed again."

"Again?" I sighed and dragged myself out of bed.

Joey wet his bed every night. He had never done that before his father died. He slept in fits and sometimes woke the house screaming from night terrors. He didn't remember them in the morning, but I did, and it tore me apart.

After some months, I attempted to go back to work. As I dropped the boys off at their kindergarten class, Joey gave me a fierce hug and said, "Goodbye, Mommy. I hope you don't die."

Stunned, I stood, coffee in hand, squeezed into a pair of pantyhose and a black pencil skirt, and stared after him as he ran off into class. I hobbled in my heels back to the car and called my boss. "I'm sorry. I won't be back in. I can't work." From then on, I chose to make life for and about them.

I signed them up for soccer, baseball, drums, dance, acting, anything and everything I could think of that would help them prosper. I took them to Disneyland, Legoland and bike riding just like we did when their daddy was alive. They might only have one parent, I thought, but I was damned if they thought it would be a handicap in any way.

During baseball, I saw the tortured look on Billy's face when the dads threw a ball with their sons. "Daddy was the best ball player," he'd say. And it was heart wrenching because it was true. His dad would have been able to teach him to play ball like no other. And had looked forward to it since the twins were babies.

It was unfair. So unfair. I couldn't teach him to throw or catch a worm burner or even the rules of the game. "I'm sorry, bud," was all I could offer.

One day, as we were driving through the windy, tree-lined path up to my parents' home in the mountains, Billy said, "Mom, if I died would I get to be with Daddy?"

The first thought that flashed through my mind was *What if I say the wrong thing and plant some sort of seed in his head to make him believe suicide will be an option when he is older*? So I quickly said, "Yes, Billy. You would see daddy, but he would be very unhappy to see you. He wants you to die when you're an old, old man so you can tell him all the exciting things about your life. You wouldn't want to make Daddy sad by missing out on watching your life, would you?"

"No," he responded, and stared out the window.

"That would make Kevin sad, too," Joey piped in.

"Kevin?" I asked.

"Yeah, God's name is Kevin. He told me. Kevin and Daddy visit me a lot when I'm sleeping. Daddy likes to come and play with me."

"Hmmm…" I said, unsure how to respond. We weren't religious. God wasn't a word I mentioned much, let alone a god named Kevin.

"Daddy comes to you in your dreams?" Billy asked Joey.

"Yeah, you just have to ask him."

Billy shrugged.

And it wasn't too long after that, I woke up from a dead sleep hearing what I thought was Joey screaming. I thought he was having another night terror. It had been a while. Both boys had been doing so well, I wondered what had set him off. But as I stepped closer to his room, I realized that the sound wasn't screaming or crying, but laughter. Loud, raucous laughter. He was sitting up in his bed, head thrown back in what had to have been the funniest thing he had ever heard.

"Joey," I whispered. "You have to go to sleep, honey."

He didn't respond.

I moved in close to him on the bottom bunk. His eyes were wide open but he saw right past me. He laughed so hard he clutched his gut and doubled over. Then he spoke some gibberish and laughed again.

"Joey," I said. But nothing. No response. Billy was sound asleep in the top bunk. How he could sleep through the noise surprised me. I laid Joey down, covered him up and left the room. I wondered then if it was true, what he said about his father coming to him and playing with him in his dreams. I prayed that it was. Wouldn't that be beautiful?

From then on, when they mentioned missing their dad, I would pull out pictures of him and tell them, "You have both parents. You have me here with you on Earth and Daddy in your heart and in Heaven. He is never away from you and you are never without Daddy."

They're happy now. The sadness and pain have faded from their eyes. Billy outgrew his suit but still has the tie. At seven, they don't remember much of their father's death two and a half years ago. Living without him has become as normal and routine as brushing their teeth twice a day. Some days they are angry and don't understand why, and on some other days they ask questions.

Today for instance, Billy asked me if his Daddy was a good man. "The best," I said.

He nodded. "So are you, Mom. You're the best, too."

"Yeah," Joey added, "We have the best Mom and Dad."

Sometimes I want to cry for what they don't have, for the things they are missing. Yet, I believe it that he is with them in their life in ways that I cannot be. In truth, I don't think he broke his promise to me at all.

He is with them and they know it.

That Day
by Heidi Morrell

On that day,
during the few before she left
for the hospital never to return,
I watched her on the day bed
struggling to be the usual part,
a mother in the yearly gathering
of her adult children,
but she barely could.
A cold wracked her already
diseased blood and bone,
she heaved for breath,
and her effort bruised me.

My eyes stole over to them
when my dad held up her limp torso,
arms lurching, head goofy like an eight week baby.
I saw them join shoulders
one a tree for the other to lean on,
and I saw his holding her steady
to comfort, to give her lungs an opening.
When I saw his head tilt down
to her putty white face,
the long love and partnership
was never clearer.

The Wardrobe
by Heidi Morrell

Some of the shirts and dresses
I don't recall,
but most of them I know well.
They span many of your Long Beach summers
and note card filled winters,
you never cared for high turnover,
if it was you, it was you.

These clothes instead reflect phases:
that era or that trip;
yes, those stripes on a visit to me,
or to a Bowl concert
in a hibiscus print jacket,
or the smart forest green velour dress
of a recent Christmas,
now treasured in a picture of you
a year before you died.

And then there's the rich blue silk blouse;
a mid-night blue that I thought made you
look like a well placed journalist
or diplomat when you dressed it up.
But hanging within inches,
are the gauzy cottons of an earth mother
that also wore Birkenstocks.

The scarves and bangles,
the loafers with New Hampshire steadiness
sewn into the leather,
the caftans celebrating patio breeziness,

all hung there like a fabric portrait.
No frame, would keep it,
no other person assemble it.
I could smell you there of course,
as my hands and fingers
examined the chapters and collars,
before it was too quickly dismantled.

The Master Gardener
by F.I. Goldhaber

All your life you took from the earth,
planting trees to feed you their fruits,
sowing seeds to reap succulent
vegetables shared with family, friends.
You grew dahlias, chrysanthemums,
roses -- food for the spirit -- to
delight your sweetie, make her smile.
You feasted from the bounty of
tomatoes, zucchini, onions,
greens, corn, beans, berries, plums, apples.
You coaxed every manner of fruits
and veggies from gardens planted
all over the country and taught
myriad others how they could
enjoy a bountiful harvest.
Now we give you back to the earth.
We pour all that remains onto
the roots of a newly planted
red oak so you may nourish
it and help it grow tall and strong.
Soon, its acorns will feed rodents
and birds. The cycle continues.

The Urn
            by F.I. Goldhaber

I search for the best display spot
for two inches filled with precious
memories from such a long life.
Lilith refuses to share space.
Stone and alabaster figures
of Bast and unknown deities
gathered from others' world journeys
withhold fitting sanctuary.
I turn to the four dragons who
menace from the most spacious ledge.
A fitting repository
for he who built rockets that sent
men into orbit, to the moon.

The Summer of My Mother's Death
by Art Heifetz

The summer of my mother's death
the pavement crackled with heat
as we waited for the rains
which never came.

We sat *shiva* at my uncle's house,
the mirrors draped in black crêpe
like the armband on my shirt.
There was a gilt-framed photo
of my mother by the door.
The men looked at it and sighed,
so pretty and so young
then clasped my father's shoulder.
His upper lip began to quiver.
The women brought
plate after plate of steaming brisket
wrapped in shiny foil.

I went down to the basement
where it was cooler
and thumbed through the Playboys
stacked against the wall.
Miss May looked like my mother.
I thought of her plump breasts
grazing my head
as she soaped me in the bath.

My uncle's collie, Lady,
put her muzzle in my lap
and disgorged a tennis ball.

I rubbed the spot behind her ears
that dogs love best
and wished that there were someone
to rub me there.

Waiting

by Craig Bradley Owens

The Veteran's Hospital doesn't smell like other hospitals I've visited. It's got a musk to it like sweat mixed with antiseptic. It also feels different. There's a sadness all around, a heaviness. Other hospitals seem to take great pains to lighten the heaviness, but not the V.A. or at least not the V.A. where my father goes for chemotherapy.

The hallways always seem dimly lit at the V.A. and the staff is friendly yet somber. This does nothing to lighten the mood. In fact, I feel the weight of the place every time I walk through the doors.

"You ready," I ask as I sit next to my father on the park bench out in front of the hospital. He's been taking to sitting on the bench for a few minutes every visit because he's too weak to walk the whole way from the parking lot to the hospital.

"Almost," he answers and presses hard on the cane between his knees. I can tell he's testing the strength of his legs. He's not strong enough to walk the next hundred feet.

He stops pressing on the cane and looks out across the hospital grounds. The humidity from the recent rain doesn't help his difficulty breathing, I know, so I sit and wait. I watch the dozens of broken men, and a few women, shuffle, stumble, or stroll past us and I contemplate the import of their differing degrees of damage.

One man, I've seen at Dad's appointments, is sitting in his motorized scooter just a few feet away. The smoke from his cigarette wafts towards us and I sigh wearily. He takes one more drag and flicks the butt off into the grass.

"I guess I better hide these," he says as he takes the pack and shoves it under the jacket in the basket fastened to the handle bars of his scooter. I can clearly see at least two other packs of cigarettes similarly concealed there. He smiles as he motors past as if to say, "Isn't that funny? A man going to chemotherapy and still hiding his smoking habit." I don't smile back. His daughter, walking behind him, shakes her head and laughs awkwardly.

A young man, maybe in his early twenties, hobbles by us on crutches. I can see the stark difference in color between his right and left leg. His right one obviously not original. He's wearing a t-shirt and shorts. Had he been standing on a street corner, I would have thought he was out jogging. The ball cap on his head bears the army logo. He doesn't smile as he passes. Instead, I see him gritting his teeth against the pain I can only assume is coming from his prosthetic. He has no one to help him cross the street, no one to lean on. I look at Dad and he begin one of his coughing fits. He pulls the paper towel, ever present in his shirt pocket now, and wipes the spittle from his mouth. I let the young man struggle past us and hope that one of the staff sees him soon.

Dad stops coughing and tries to hide the paper towel before I see the blood stain. I look away to allow him to believe he succeeded. He tries to inhale and I can hear the fluttering of something not quite attached in his chest. A young couple walk past holding hands. They look even younger than the man on the crutches. They both walk freely, they seem strong, but I know that I will see them back in the chemotherapy waiting room later today. I've seen them there before, just once, and I worry that the strength I see in this young man will not be there after today.

"You ready?" Dad asks and rises to his feet. I get up and follow him, measuring my steps so that I keep pace with him. I'm struck by the family joke me and my mother share whenever we go shopping with Dad. "He just leaves me," my mother would say as I walked with her and we both would watch my father with his long, powerful strides increasing the distance between us so rapidly that we barely had time to get out of the car before he was in the store. Today is different. Today, I have to pause after every other step to allow my father to catch up.

I walk a little bit ahead to open the door to the building. I wait as he walks inside. I can tell that he's concentrating on taking individual steps and not shuffling. I don't know why he bothers, but I'm glad that he does.

Inside, that heady musk greets us like an unwelcome visitor. The heavy silence pools at our feet as we walk slowly, purposefully to the first waiting room. Dad takes a number off the wall. He's number three and I wonder if it bothers him that he couldn't be first today. He always tries to be first. Recently, his number has been getting higher.

"Number one," the woman who takes the blood calls out from the open door of the blood lab. A man steps to the door. I can't tell what brought him to the V.A. today. I hope it's just for a checkup.

"Do you have a hearing test today?" I ask as we wait for number one to get finished.

"Yeah, at 10:00," Dad answers. There's a whirring noise coming from the hall just behind us and I know that the custodians are cleaning the floors. They are always running the floor polishers this early, before anyone other than my father and the two who beat him arrive.

"Number two," the woman calls and another man goes to the door. He looks even healthier than number one. I'm happy for them both.

"I hope they don't have that chicken salad again," Dad says and I know what he expects me to say.

"I'll go out and get you something. What do you want?"

"A chicken breast and a biscuit," he says and I knew that would be his answer. Sometimes it's a hot dog with sauerkraut. On those days, I can just go to the cafeteria. I knew today he would want fried chicken, which they do not serve at the hospital.

"Number three," the woman calls and dad struggles to his feet. He goes to the door and waits a moment before heading back to the chair where she draws the blood. I wait to get up until he's all the way next to me and we walk back to the chemotherapy waiting room. Sure enough, the young couple is sitting there. So is the man on the scooter with the hidden cigarettes. The wait here is not long. They need to get the saline started soon so that they can get the chemo started by the afternoon. The waiting room empties as the patients disappear. I sit and watch the cigarette man's daughter start her knitting and I watch the young woman begin to pace up and down the halls. I open the Kindle book on my phone and start to read.

After a trip to the cafeteria for a soda and a couple of trips to the bathroom, when my book has lost its interest to me, and I lament that the hospital walls block signals so I can't download another, after I've checked on Dad at least three times, and after a parade of people come in and out of the room, it's nearly time for Dad's hearing test. I head back to the chemotherapy room. Dad is in the same chair he's always in--the furthest from the door. He's watching the television on the swiveling arm attached to his chair.

Dad is already up and holding onto his i.v. stand. He rolls in past me and into the hall. "Let's go," he says, and I follow.

The auditory lab is one floor down so we take the elevator.

"Press one," he instructs and I want to say that I know which floor. I've been to the same floor every visit. I don't say anything. I press the number one and think back to when I used to beg to press the elevator buttons. We get to the small waiting room down a long hallway and I take a seat under the television. Dad checks in and sits next to me. We wait together.

"You taking chemo?" an ancient looking man asks loudly from a seat directly across from us.

"Yeah, I'm on my third treatment. Already had forty radiation treatments. Now, I'm doing chemo," Dad says in that scratchy voice that is all he can muster since the tumor is still partly in his throat.

The man nods politely even though I can tell he couldn't hear a word Dad said. The room falls into silence.

"Owens," a woman calls as she pokes her head out from behind a door.

"Yep," Dad rasps and pushes against his cane until he stands. They disappear behind the door. I pull out my phone and open my book. I read the same sentence three times and close the program. There's even less of a signal down here in the basement, if it's possible to have less than nothing. I sit and listen to the television above my head. I can see and bathroom across the hall and I go even though I really don't have to. I read the posters and the bulletin board posts. Evidently, there's a seminar called, "Living Well with Cancer" next week. I find that a cruel joke. I memorize the inner workings of the human ear as it is outlined on a poster in my line of sight. I also learn that hearing is intimately tied to emotion. Whenever you hear a sound with an emotional attachment, you will actually feel the emotion. I find that bit of information irritating as I sit amid the all-consuming silence of this room.

I can hear Dad's voice, raspy and weak, approaching the door so I stand and wait. He comes out and we head back to the elevator.

"See you at lunch," I say as he goes back to the chair farthest from the door. I go back into the waiting room. The room is emptier than before. Someone has switched off the television and I make it a point to turn it back on immediately. The only thing worse than the drone of daytime television in this room is the silence. I pick up a magazine. I've read it before. I pick up another. Nothing of interest. I pick up another. Boring. I pick up another. Read it. I go to a different table. There's a Reader's Digest from the 80's there. I take it and read about a man who was lost in the arctic for nearly a month and I peruse some mildly amusing anecdotes from real people. I learn how to grill watermelon. Who knew you could grill watermelon? I'm fascinated with the concept. Wouldn't it dry out? Isn't watermelon mostly water? Has someone really figured out how to grill water? And if they've been grilling water since the 80's, why am I just now hearing about it? It's nearly lunchtime by the time I stop thinking about grilled watermelon. I head back to the chemotherapy room.

Dad's in his same chair. I walk up to him.

"What do they have for lunch?" I ask, knowing that it will be chicken salad.

"Hey, Sherri," Dad yells toward the little office across from him. "What's for lunch?"

"I think, chicken salad," Sherri answers.

"I'll go out and get you something," I say as he winces. I leave the room and walk quickly out and to the parking lot. The traffic has picked up so it takes me a little while to get into the flow and leave the hospital. I head across the street to the Bojangles. When I get back, there are no more parking spaces. I finally find a space next to the walking trail and I know that I'll have a long walk to the hospital and a long walk to get the car while Dad waits on the park bench, but I don't mind. The humidity of the morning has lifted and the day is bright and sunny. There's a breeze blowing that brings the smell of pine and some flower that I can't identify. I stroll effortlessly through the park and onto the roadway leading to the hospital. I walk past Dad's bench and into the building. The air conditioning hits me like a cold slap. I would prefer to sit outside. I think that I might be able to go for a walk this afternoon. Dad has nothing scheduled that I know of, but I know that I won't. I'll just sit in the waiting room.

I take the chicken breast and biscuit back to Dad and wait until I'm sure he doesn't need anything else before I go back to waiting. The room is quiet again. Someone has turned off the television. I turn it back on. I take out my phone and realize I didn't download another book while I was out. I've got to remember to do that. I guess I could go for a walk and download a book. I should go for a walk. I can. Nothing will happen. No one will even know I was gone. I can. Instead, I head to the cafeteria for a soda.

The smell of the food in the warming trays makes my stomach tighten and I realize I haven't eaten today. I look over the food. Nothing looks good to me, but I order a veggie sub anyway. I grab a soda and get in line to pay. There are two women working. The same two who are there when Dad wants a hot dog. I pick the one I know to be more friendly and I wait even though the other line is moving faster.

I arrive back at the waiting room to the sounds of Spongebob emanating from the television and I realize a family has taken up residence in my usual spot. I don't mind. I head to the other side of the room, as far away from the flashing colors and playful music as I can get. I eat my sub and drink my soda. I kick myself for not checking for service when I was in the cafeteria and I open my book and close it again. I go to the bathroom, walk down to the information desk and back. I read an entertainment magazine and try to determine why one actress wore the exact same dress better than another, figure it's the camera angles and the bias of the reporter because I see no difference. I open the music files on my phone and plug in my headphones. I play some songs and close my eyes.

The familiar tunes drift in and out of me with playful accuracy. I let the music take me to a better place and I linger there. I feel happier, lighter, freer, and I can't believe that damn poster in the basement was right about sound being tied to emotion. I try to make a mental note to bring my iPod to the next treatment. Maybe that will help pass the time. Or I could download another book before then. I start to feel frustrating and impatient and I realize my music has stopped. I just don't have that many songs on my phone. I think about replaying them but I don't.

I get up and walk to every table in the large room. There are no magazines I want to read. I look at the clock next to the television. Just three more hours.

Then, I play the game I always do when I watch the clock. I start counting the seconds and I look away while I continue counting. I count for a while then I look back to see how well I kept time. I try and do the math to tally up my score and I try to count again. A full minute this time. Then, I tally, which takes another minute. Then, I count again. And again. And again. I start to think about stories I could be writing. It takes until the late afternoon for my mind to realize that I could have brought my laptop and written a novel by now. I add my laptop to the list of things to bring next time.

The daughter of cigarette hider is still sitting in the same chair as when I noticed her this morning. Has she moved? The scarf she's knitting looks almost complete. I don't recall how far along she was this morning. I wonder if I should take up knitting. She looks so calm.

"Let's go," Dad suddenly says next to me.

"You done?" I ask stupidly. He's already walking down the hall toward the door. I take my time but I catch up quickly. He sits on the bench as I go get the car. It's late afternoon and the breeze is gone. It's hot and sticky. I hurry to the car and pick Dad up. We head out of the hospital and I can't wait to get home and take a nap.

The Wave Goodbye
by Robert E. Petras

I remember the way my Mom stood
In the doorway before her memory failed,
One arm clutched around her waist,
The other waving a hand,
A wave with the slightest reach, a gentle touch,
The way a new mother first touches her child.
I could see in the rearview mirror she was still waving
As I wheeled around the corner,
The same way she stood
Behind the window of the nursing home
Through the opaque nylon curtain
Through the slats of the blinds
Through the mirrored years.
Her wave still touches me.

Author & Poet Biographies

Madeline Beckwith is a spoken word poet, singer, author, patient advocate, karaoke jockey, kick-ass poker player, and staunch supporter of the Oxford comma. Although originally from Nebraska, she considers Las Vegas to be her artistic home. She was the Las Vegas Grand Slam Champion in 2002 and came in 2nd in 2003. She hosted Las Vegas' first weekly poetry slam in conjunction with Clark County Parks and Recreation before branching out to other venues. She has toured across the country in support of my first CD: "What It's Like for Girls." Her second spoken word effort, dedicated to the staff of the University of Nebraska and her family for helping her heal gracefully from a long hospital stay, is called "UNfinished. You can check out selected tracks at www.reverbnation.com/MadelineBeckwith

Rick Blum has been writing prose and poetry for more than 25 years during stints as a nightclub owner, high-tech manager, market research mogul and, most recently, alter kaker. His essays and poems have appeared in *The Boston Globe, Humor Times, Breath and Shadow*, and *The Muddy River Poetry Review* among others. He was recently named winner of the 2014 Carlisle Poetry Contest. Currently, he is holed up in his office in Massachusetts trying to pen the perfect bio, which he plans to share as soon as he stops laughing at the sheer futility of this effort.

Tina V. Cabrera earned her MFA in Fiction from San Diego State University in 2009. She is currently completing her PhD in English & Creative Nonfiction at the University of North Texas. Excerpts from her novel, short fiction, and poetry have appeared in journals such as *Quickly, Crack the Spine, Big Bridge Magazine, Vagabondage Press, San Diego Poetry Annual, Fiction International* and *Outrider Press.* She has presented critical work at the Northeast Modern Language Association (NeMLA) in New

York and Pennsylvania, which has been published in print and online. You can visit her writer's blog at www.cannyuncanny.wordpress.com

FERN G. Z. CARR is a lawyer, teacher and past president of the Society for the Prevention of Cruelty to Animals. A member of and former Poet-in-Residence for the League of Canadian Poets, she composes and translates poetry in five languages. Carr is a 2013 Pushcart Prize nominee and has been cited as a contributor to the Prakalpana literary movement in India. She has been published extensively world-wide from Finland to the Seychelles. Some of her poetry was assigned reading for a West Virginia University College of Law course entitled "Lawyers, Poets, and Poetry".
  Canadian honours include: an online feature in *The Globe and Mail,* Canada's national newspaper; poetry set to music by a Juno-nominated musician; and her poem, "I Am", chosen by the Parliamentary Poet Laureate as Poem of the Month for Canada. One of Carr's haiku is even included on a DVD sent to Mars on NASA's MAVEN spacecraft. See more about Fern at www.fernzcarr.com

Sean Davis is the author of *The Wax Bullet War* and his work has appeared in various online and print magazines and periodicals such as *Flaunt Magazine*, *The Willamette Week* and many others. He currently lives in NE Portland, Oregon.

As a reporter, editor, business writer, and marketing communications consultant, **F.I. Goldhaber** produced words for newspapers, corporations, governments, and non-profits. Now, her poems, short stories, novelettes, essays, and reviews appear in paper, electronic, and audio magazines, ezines, newspapers, calendars, and anthologies. Her fourth poetry collection, *Subversive Verse*, released in October. www.goldhaber.net

Art Heifetz teaches ESL to refugees in Richmond, Va. In 2013, he won second prize in the Reuben Rose poetry competition in Israel. He has had over 170 poems published in 13 countries. See www.polishedbrasspoems.com for more of his work.

Debi Knight Kennedy is a writer, sculptor and member of the puppet troupe "Geppetto's Junkyard", living the small town dream in Haines, Alaska. Her writing can be found in the NPR anthology *This I Believe—On Love*, the zine *Glacial Misbehavior* and the UAS Literary Journal *Tidal Echoes*. Debi's art is scattered throughout Alaska, the Pacific Northwest and the world in galleries, private collections and museums.

Francis X. LaChapelle is from Oregon. He received his MA from Stanford University as a National Science Graduate Research Fellow. His poems have appeared in *DMQ Review*.

Adam Loewen was born in Missoula, Montana, and received an Economics Degree from the University of Montana before finding a home in Portland, Oregon. His only novel, *The Revelation Complex*, is currently seeking representation. Adam has directed and starred in two films, *Going With the Flow (2010)* and *Accidance! (2015)*. As Head of sales for Stein Unlimited, Adam manages and fronts a corporate entity which performs conceptual rock music about sex, dreams, and the philosophy of dualism. At present, Adam runs an art household in Southwest Portland called The Flophouse and teaches children's music classes.

Katey Lovell is a writer of poetry and fiction, usually about relationships. Her short stories have appeared in magazines and anthologies. Katey lives in South Yorkshire, UK, with her husband David and their son, Zachary.

Heidi Morrell lives in Los Angeles, is married and lives in a big old house with her two kids, patient husband, one dog and two cats. Formerly an actress and short film maker, she stopped that because of a muscular neuropathy. No matter, she's been ardently writing since age nine, but only in the last three years began to submit her work to the wider world. Some of those publications include magazines, anthologies and e-zines, among them: *East Coast literary Review, Poised in Flight Anthology, Hurricane Press, Emerge Literary Journal, Poetry Pacific, Rotary Dial, Canadian, Outside In Lit&Travel Magazine,* and a forthcoming Chapbook from Finishing Line Press. She also writes short stories several of which have been published.

Rene Mullen has a Master's degree from the University of Wisconsin at Milwaukee. His fiction can be found in *Black Mirror Magazine* and *94 Creations*, and his nonfiction can be found in *Inclusion* and the *Albanian Journal of Politics*. In his spare time, he travels small town America in search of new experiences.

Craig Bradley Owens, originally from a small town in the coalfields of Virginia, now lives in Johnson City, TN. He currently works as an Assistant Professor of English at Walters State Community College in Morristown, TN. His work has appeared in *The Dead Mule School of Southern Literature, Black Mirror Magazine,* and *Leaves of Ink.*

Miriam Pederson lives in Grand Rapids, Michigan where she is a Professor Emeritus of English at Aquinas College. She earned an MFA degree in Creative Writing from Western Michigan University. Her chapbook, *This Brief Light*, was published in 2003 by Finishing Line Press. Her poetry has been published in many anthologies, journals, and small press magazines including *New Poems from the Third Coast: Contemporary Michigan Poetry* (anthology), *The MacGuffin, Passages North, The Book of Birth*

Poetry (anthology), *Christianity and Literature, Sing Heavenly Muse,* and *Song of the Owastanong: Grand Rapids Poetry in the 21ˢᵗ Century.* Pederson's poems in collaboration with sculpture created by her husband, Ron Pederson, are exhibited in area and regional galleries documented in three collections of collaborative images and poems: *The Adding We Do in Our Sleep, Doubletake,* and *Evidence of Things Unseen.*

Robert E. Petras is a graduate of West Liberty State University and a resident of Toronto, Ohio. His fiction and poetry have appeared in more than 170 publications.

Susan Pierce is writer from Northern CA, avid yoga practitioner and runner. She's performed fiction and memoir work as part of Unchaste Readers and Penduline Reading Series. Currently, she is working on her second historical fiction novel.

Judith Pulman writes poetry and prose in Portland, Oregon where she also translates poems from Russian to English, just to keep things light. She has been published in or has work forthcoming from *The Writer's Chronicle, Los Angeles Review, Brevity, New Ohio Review,* and *Basalt.* She works as a teacher, administrator, and editor. Find out more about her at www.judithpulman.com

Kate Redmond repatriated to the United States in 2010 after seventeen years living overseas in Central Asia, the Caucasus, the Horn of Africa and Indonesia. She has worked as a writer and editor for dozens of international organizations. Now she writes essays and fiction in Portland, Oregon.

Claudia F. Savage has been a chef for people recovering from illness, a book editor, and a teacher of poetry, but her most challenging and joyous job is as mother to her two-year-old daughter, River Amira. Her poems and interviews have recently been in *CutBank, The Denver Quarterly, Iron Horse Review, The Buddhist Poetry Review, Cordella*, and *Bookslut.* As a poet, she's been awarded residencies at Ucross, Jentel, and the Atlantic Center for the Arts where she met her husband, an experimental jazz flutist and saxophonist. Their duo, THrum, creates and performs throughout the Pacific Northwest. Musings and collaborations can be found at www.whilethe riversleeps.com and in her column about balancing parenting and art-making, "Leave the Dishes," at VoiceCatcher.com

Emily Shearer lives, writes, and teaches yoga in Prague, Czech Republic, with her husband and three children. She lost her mother in 1998 after a six-year battle with ovarian cancer. Her poetry has been published in *ROAR* (forthcoming), *LiteraryMama.com, writing the whirlwind, Mercury Retrograde* (from Kattywhompus Press), and *Minerva Rising*, where she is the Poetry Editor. You can read more of her work and view her photo albums at www.lineupyourducks.com

Jessica Standifird is a writer, editor and musician. She is co-founder of Blue Skirt Productions, plays in the band Bright & Shiny, and dabbles in the visual arts. She is awful at writing bios. www.blueskirtproductions.com
www.pageofjess.com

~~~

Sally K Lehman is the author of *Small Minutes, The Unit—Room 154,* and *Living in the Second Tense,* which are available for purchase for Kindle on Amazon, and the editor of the anthology *Bear the Pall.* She has had poetry and short stories published in several literary magazines including *Bewildering Stories, Ascent Aspirations, The Scruffy Dog Review, Voice Catchers, Perceptions: a Magazine of the Arts,* and *Lunch Ticket.* She has a web site for current projects at www.SallyKLehman.com and was a founding member of the artisan collective Blue Skirt Productions. Sally studied Mathematics at UC Berkeley and worked in the computer industry for many years prior to becoming a full time writer. She currently lives in the Portland, Oregon area.

Cover photograph by **Jessica Standifirid**

39779638R00065

Made in the USA
Charleston, SC
20 March 2015